SCAN THIS BOOK

Compiled by John Mende

ART DIRECTION BOOK COMPANY

ISBN: 0-88108-099-3
Library of Congress Catalog Number: 91-077465

Printed in the United States of America.

Published by:
Art Direction Book Company
10 East 39th Street
New York, New York 10016

Typeset by Magee Graphic Corp., San Luis Obispo, California.

Using This Book

Unlike other clip art collections, the common objects in this book have been selected because they are not readily identifiable as belonging to any particular period in history. They should therefore be of greater value for use in a wide variety of graphic design and advertising applications. These images have been chosen for a thickness of line which makes them suitable for use with even the most inexpensive desktop scanners, though they are ideal for photostating and photocopying as well.

If the object you select is to be reproduced in a desktop publishing program such as Aldus Pagemaker or Quark Xpress, scan as line art at a resolution determined by the quality of output required. For example, artwork that is to be laserprinted requires much lower resolution and less memory (125 dots per inch) than final Linotronic output (300 dpi or greater). When scanning, always remember to save the image in the file format compatible with the software that you will be using.

If a photographic manipulation program such as Adobe Photoshop is available, the images in this book can be customized using the special effects built into this type of software. Scan as gray scale art for greatest flexibility in altering the object; color may be added by converting the gray scale file to RGB or CMYK. If the ultimate output of your work is a color separation, scan at the highest dpi possible. For other color applications, such as a Canon Laser Copier or HP Paintwriter, consult your operating manual or service bureau for specific dpi and file format recommendations before scanning.

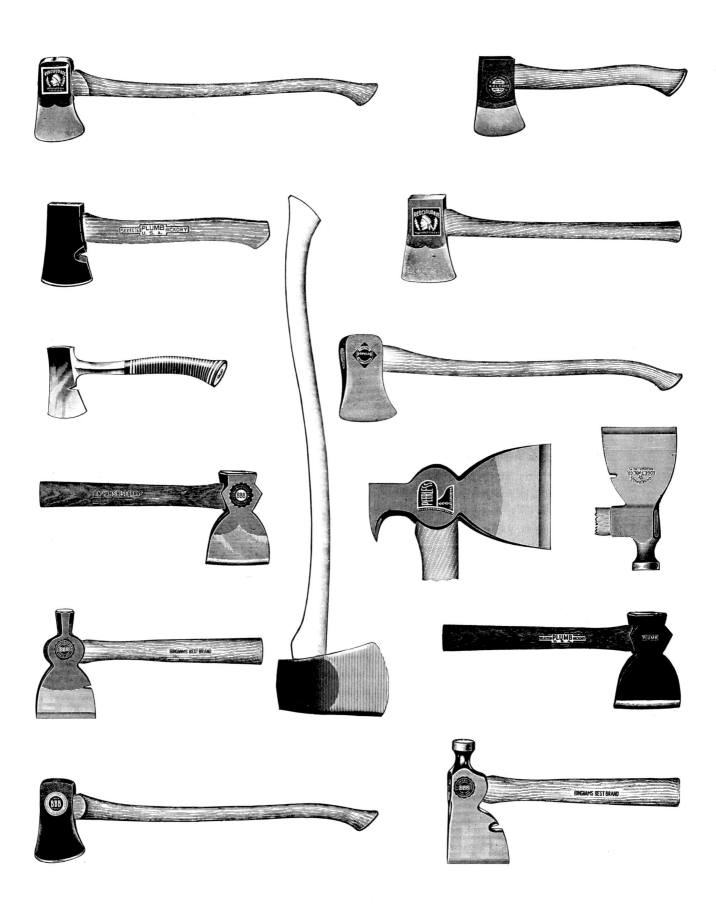

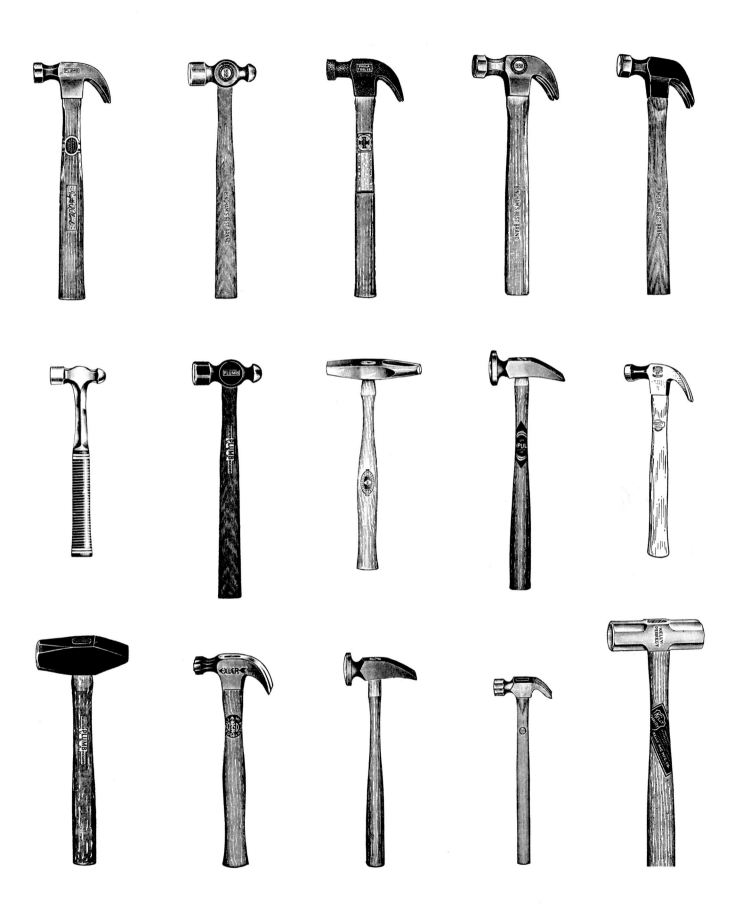

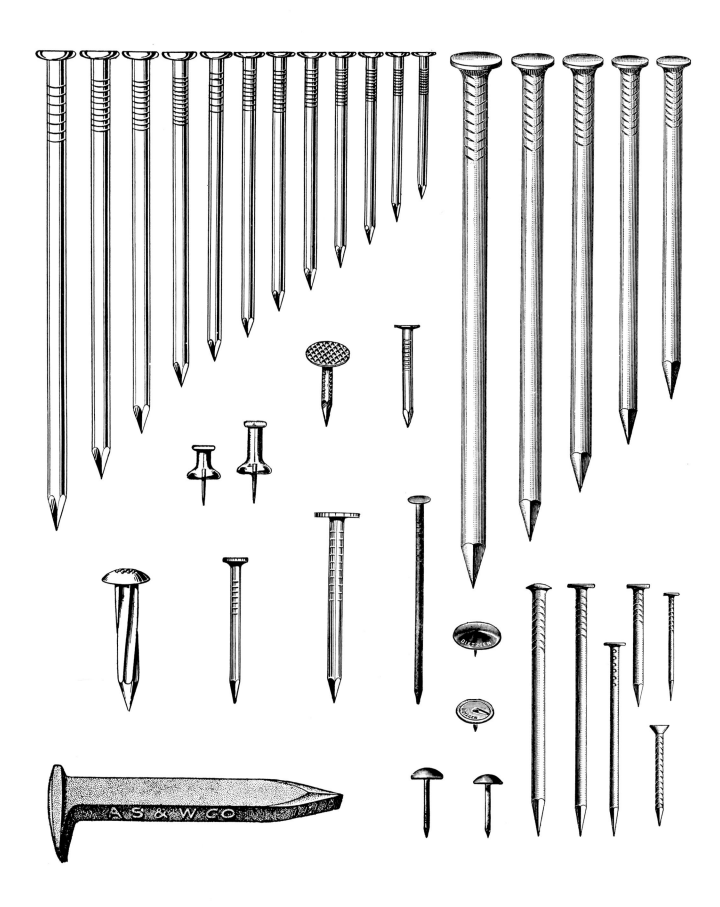

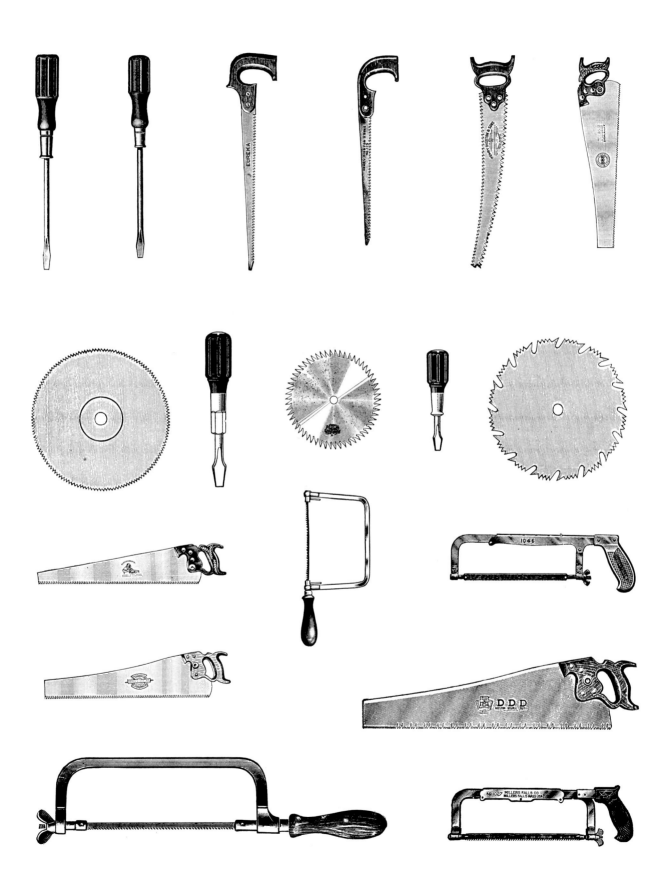

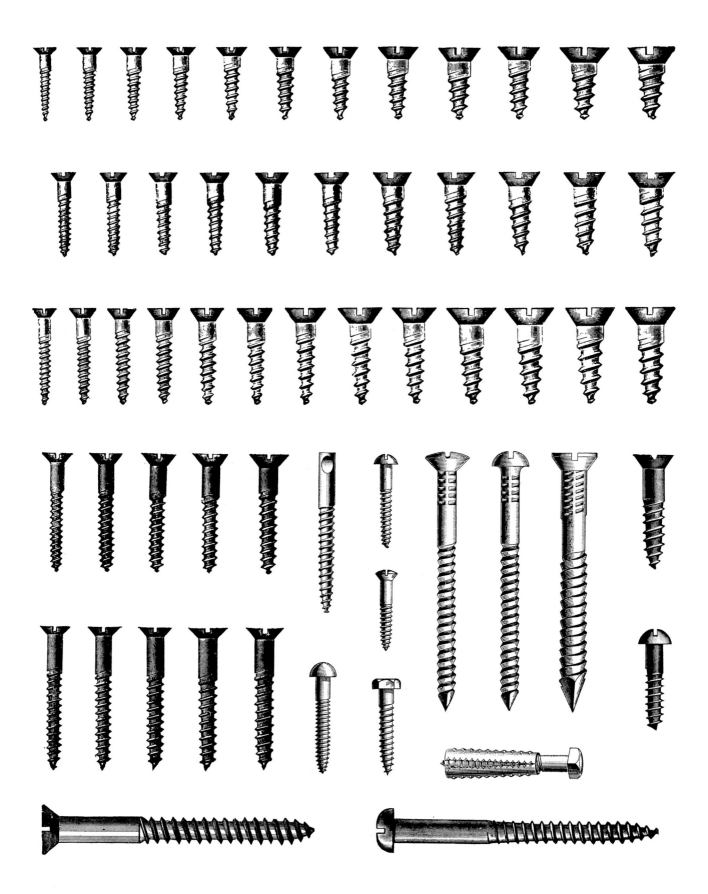

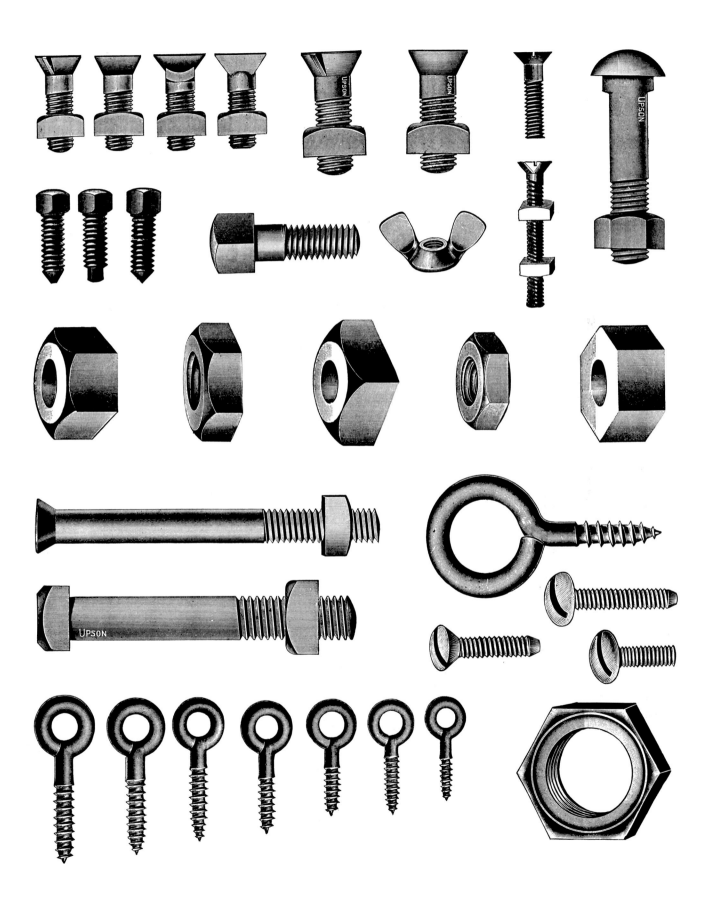

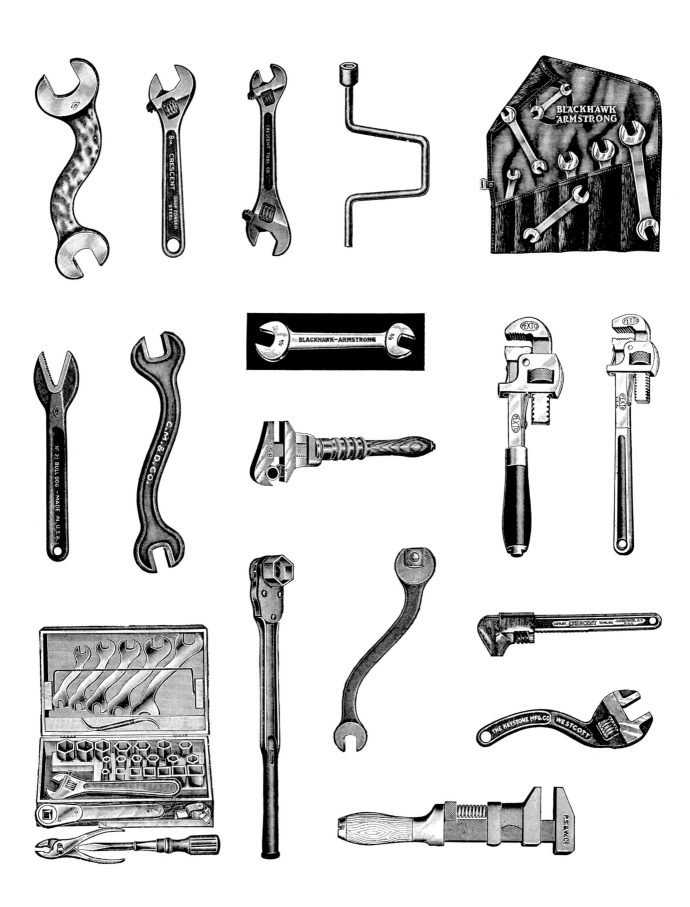

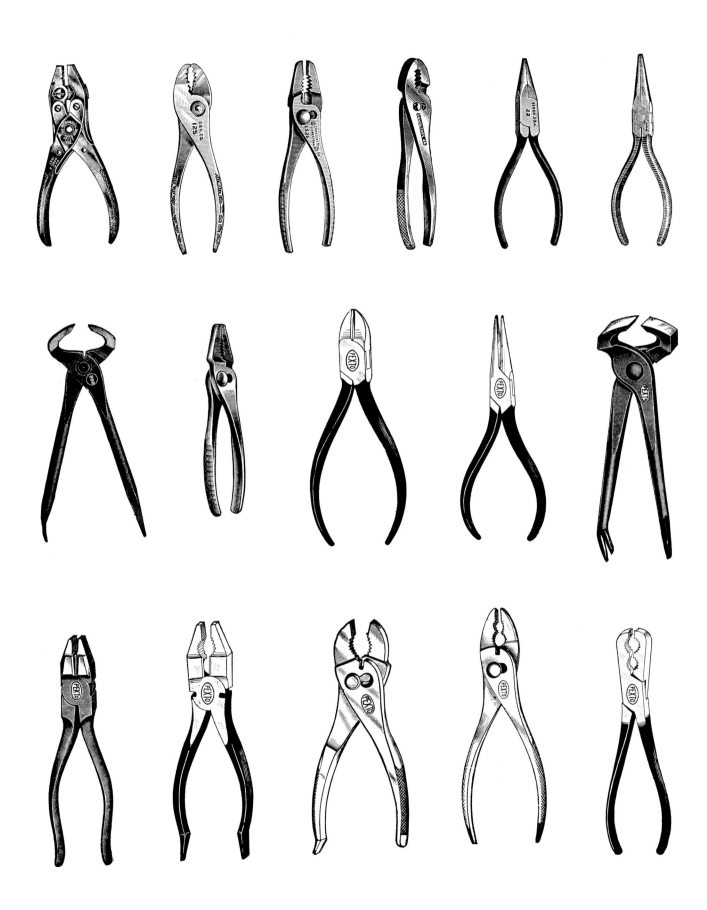

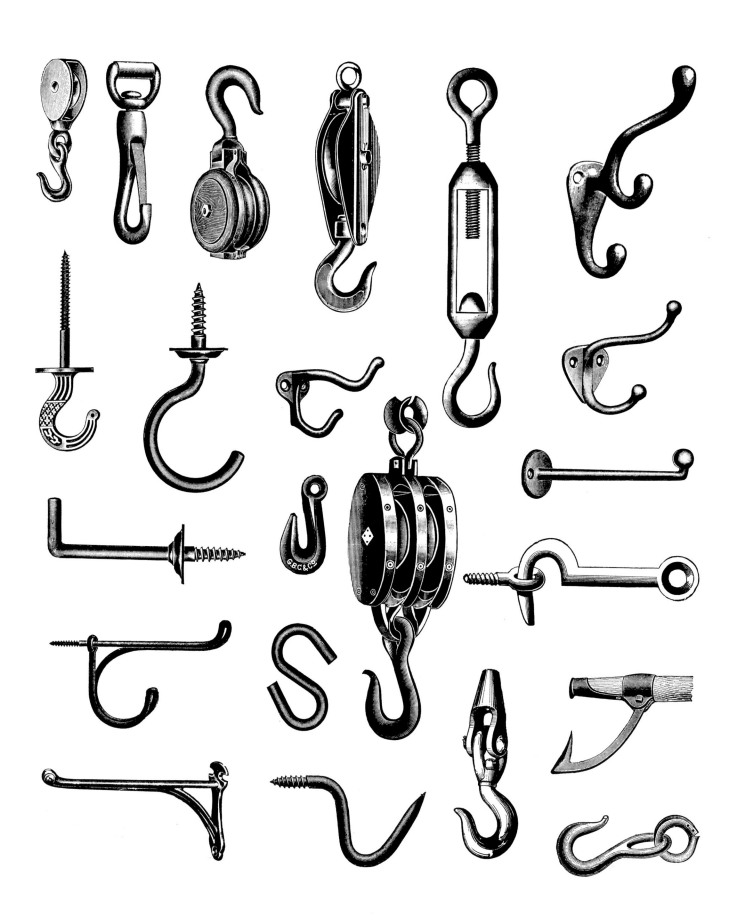

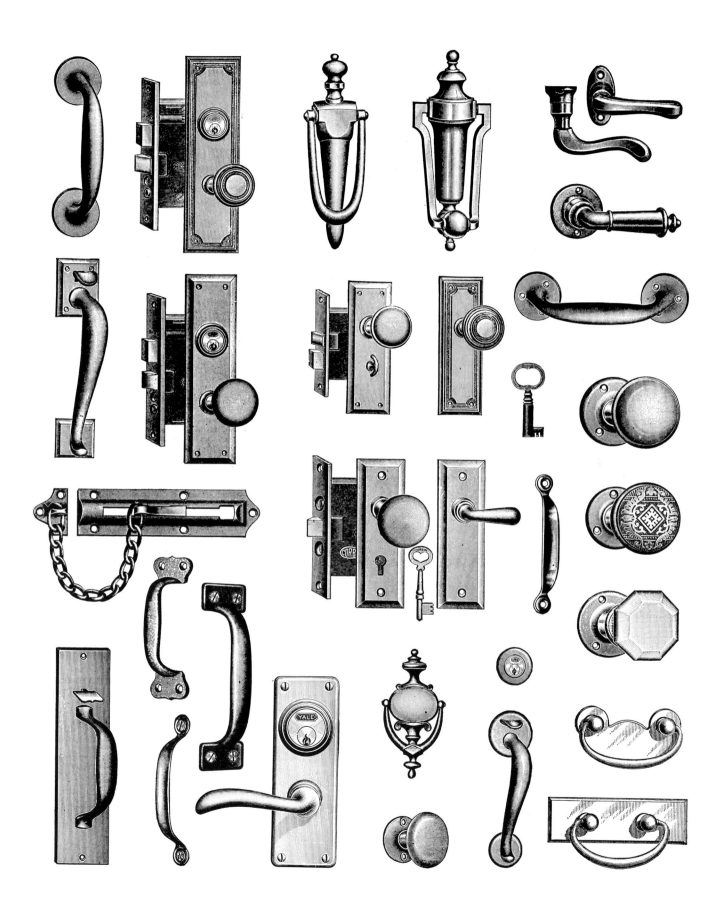

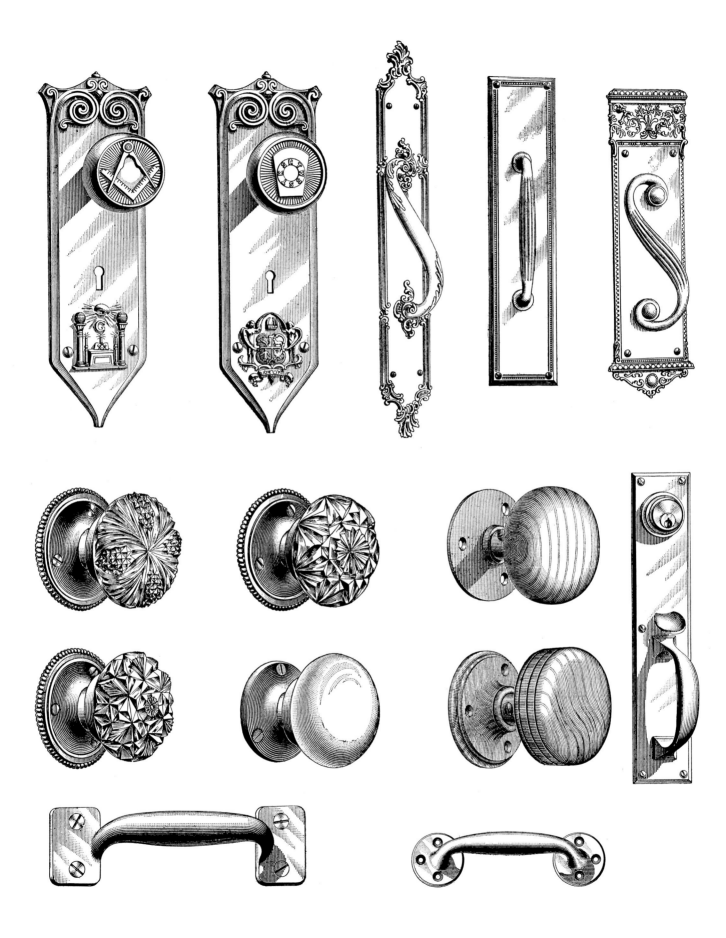

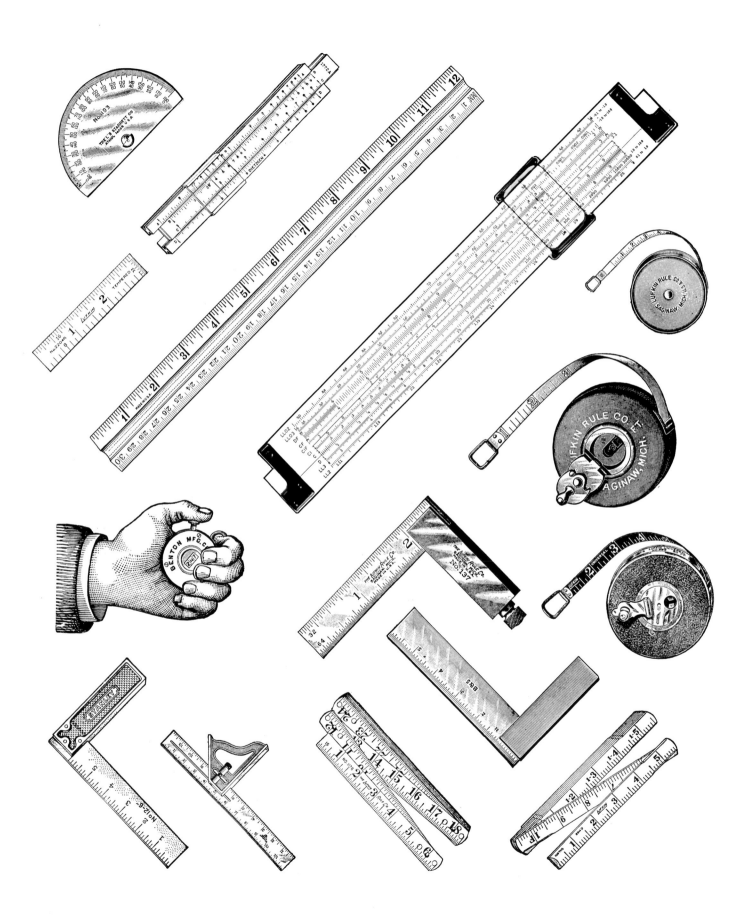

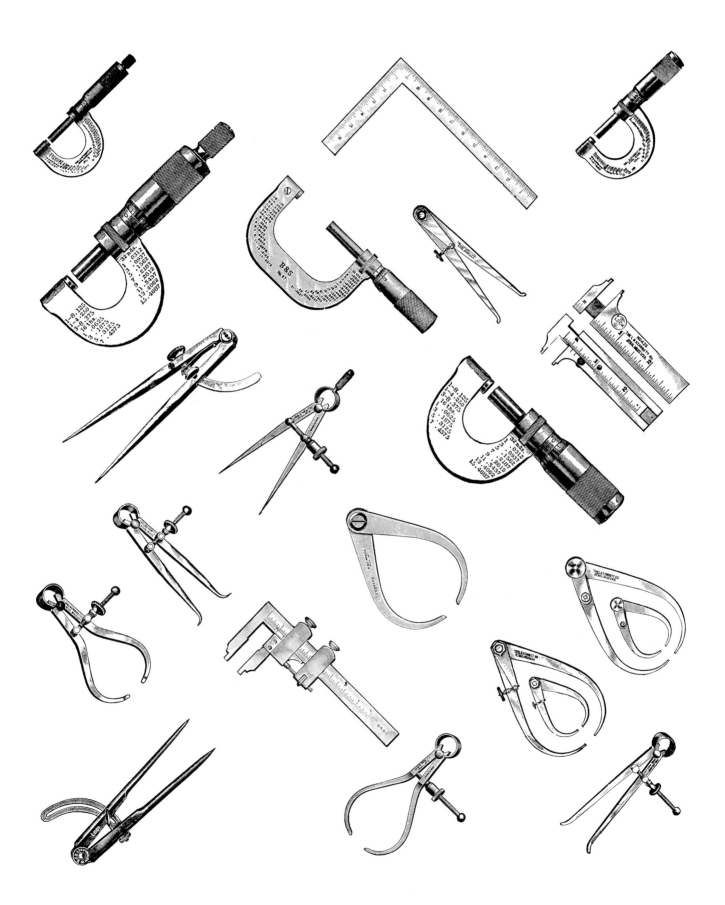

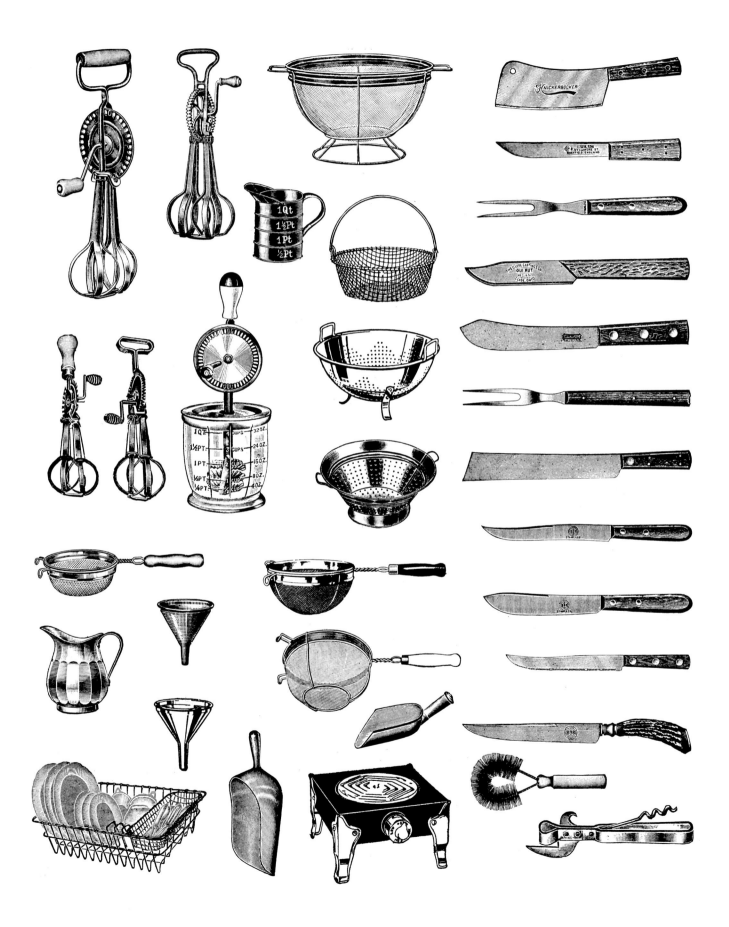

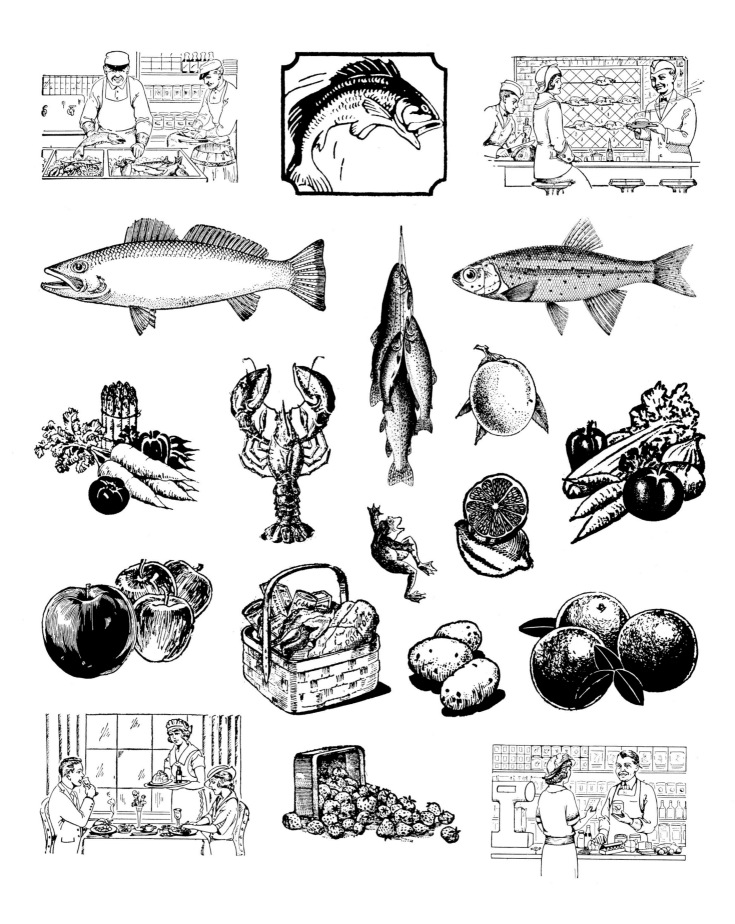

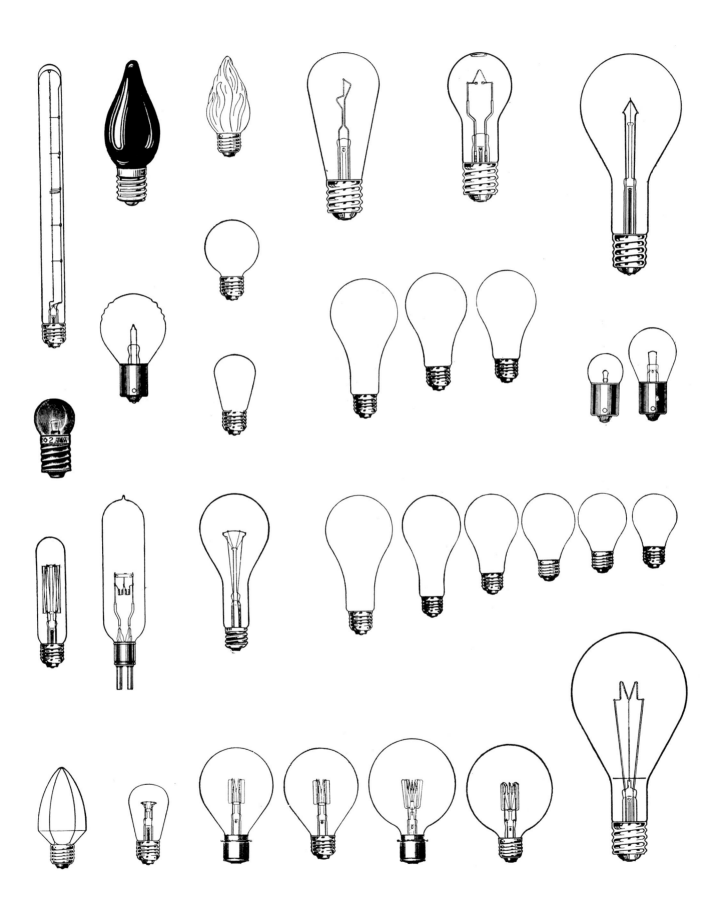

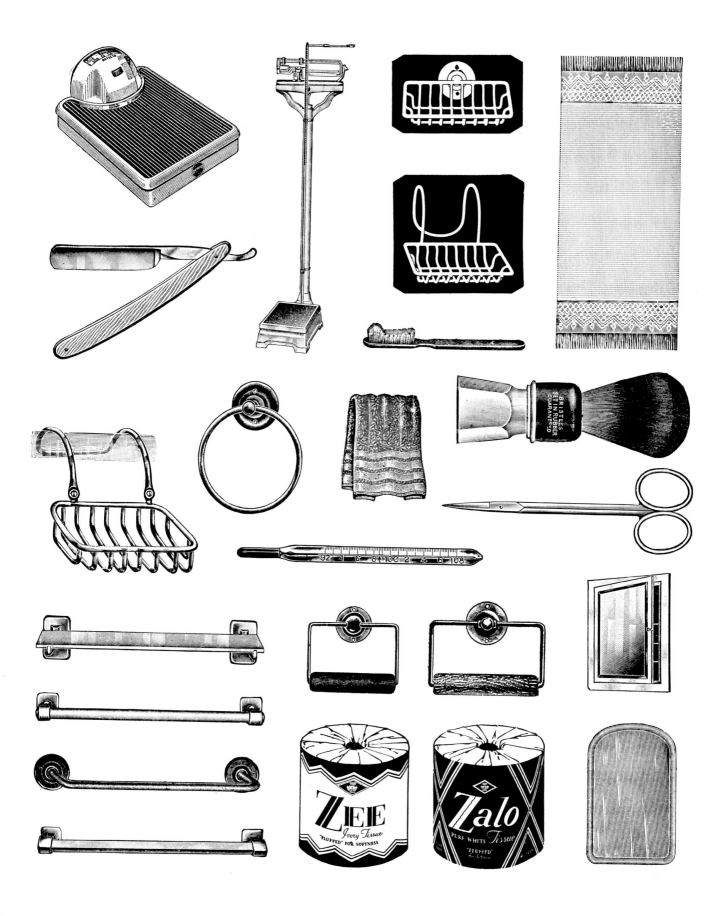

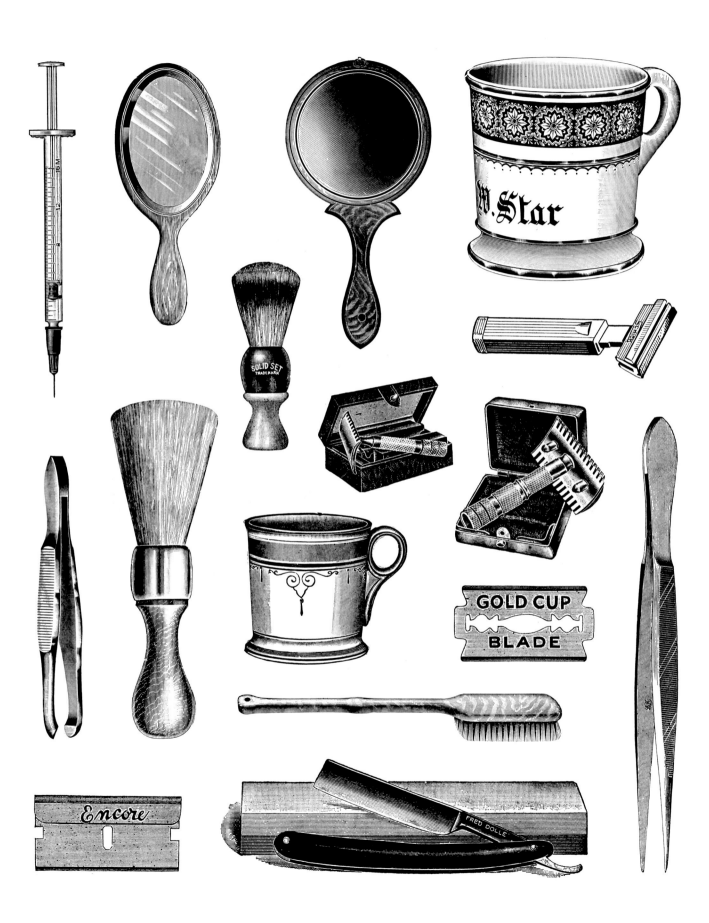

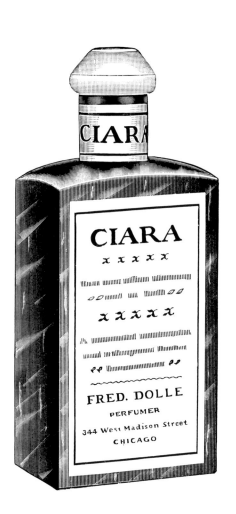

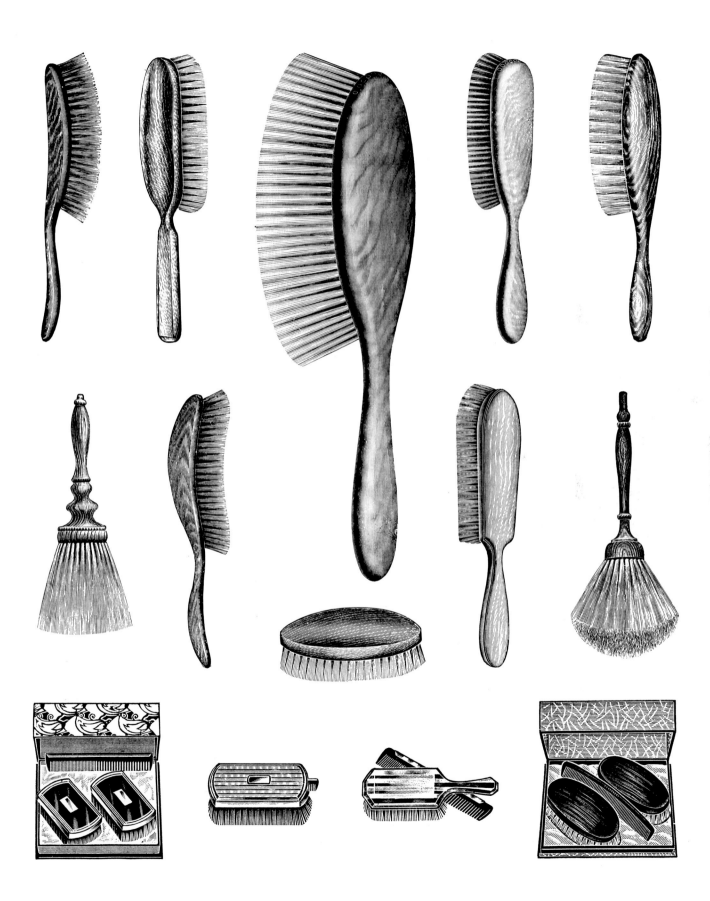

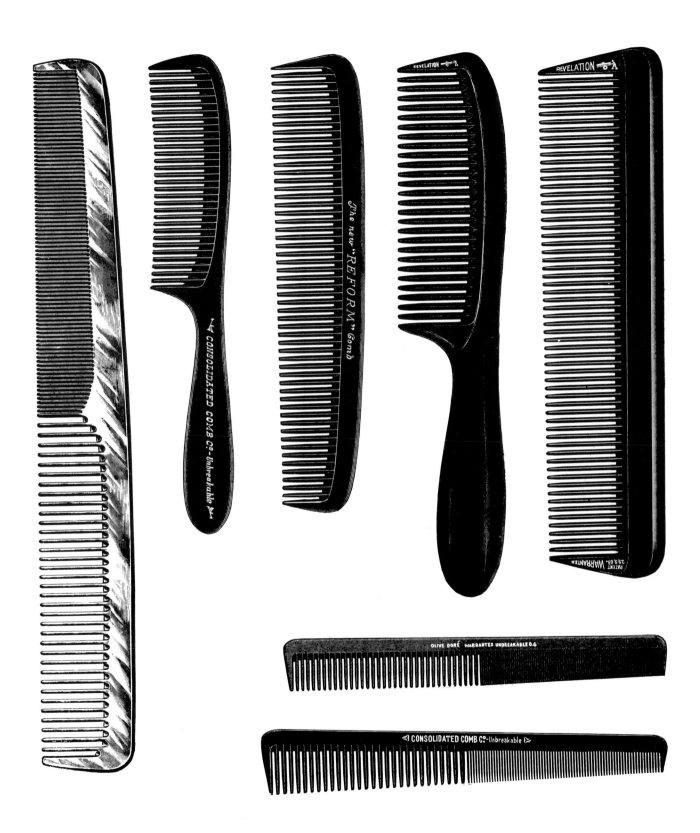

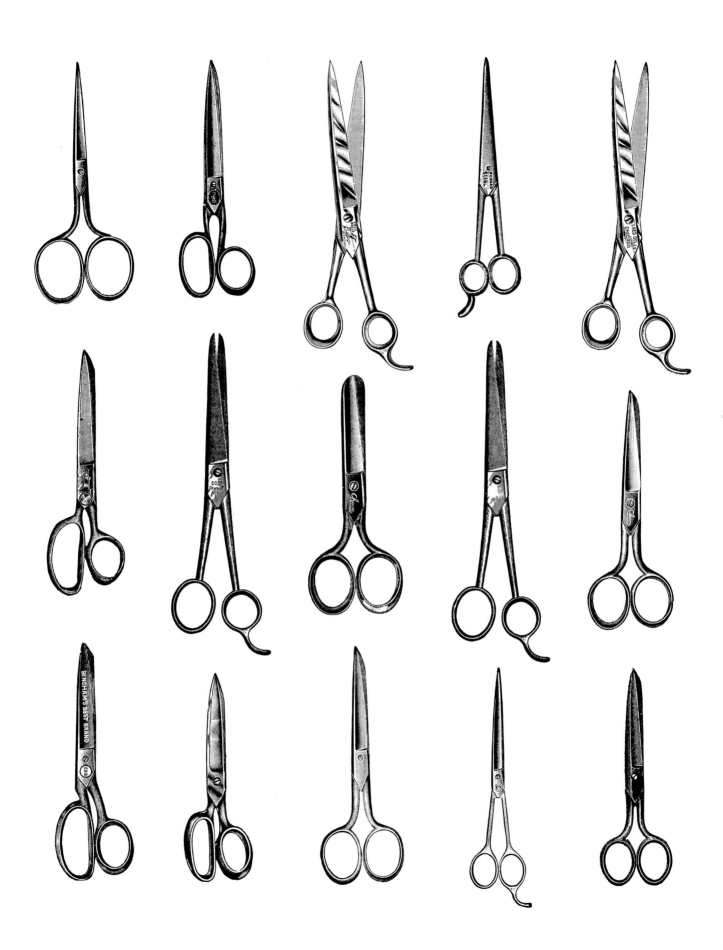

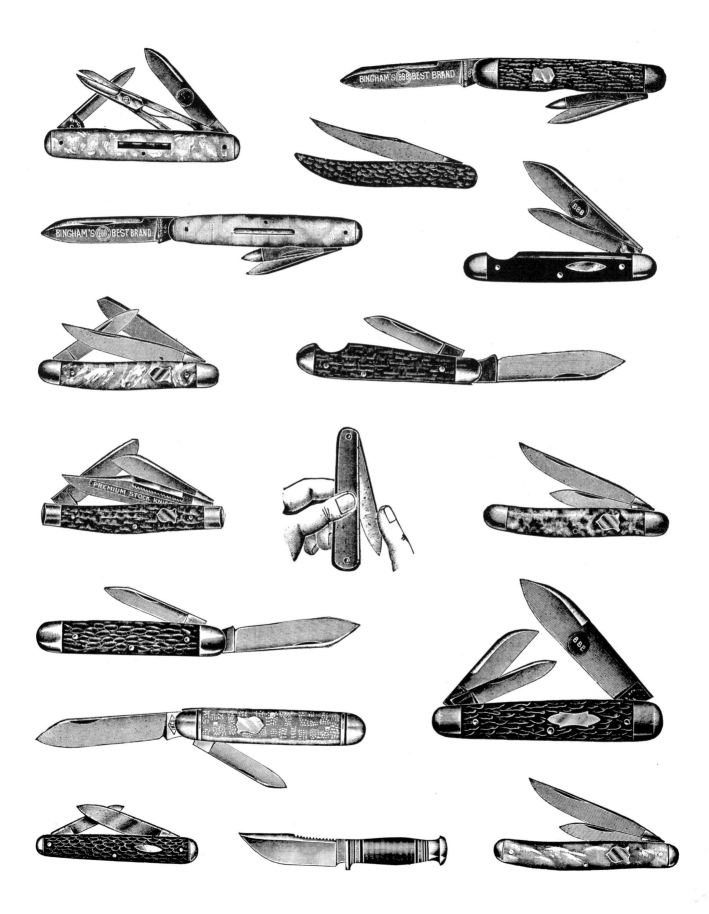

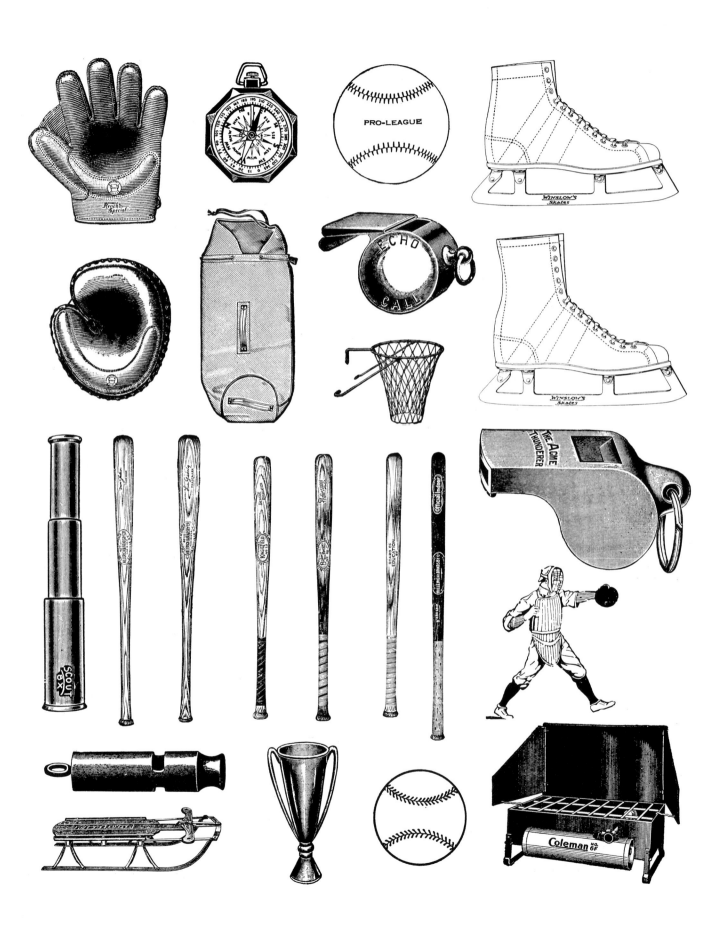

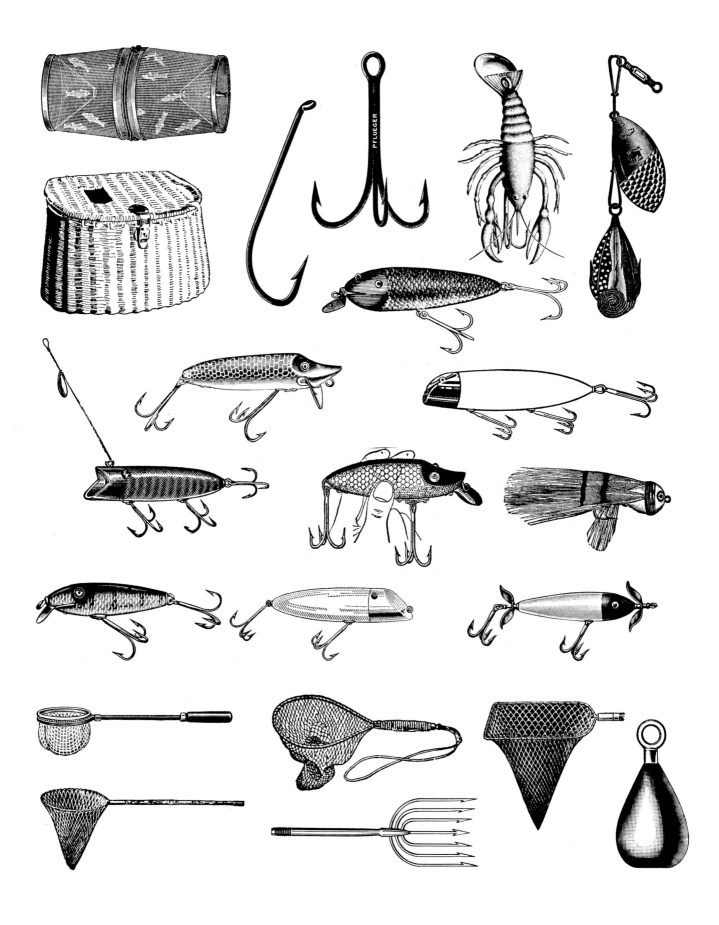

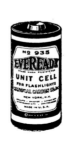

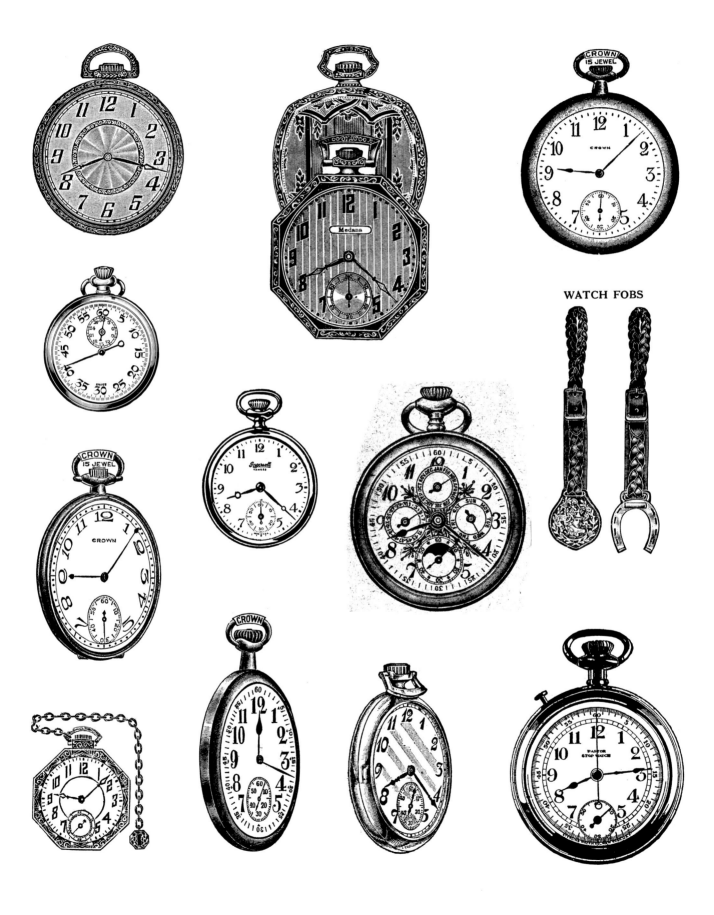

WATCH FOBS

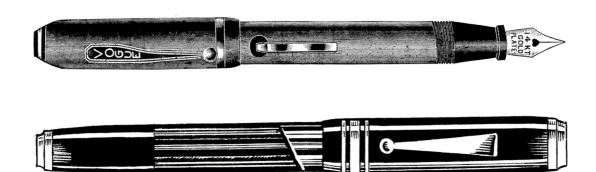

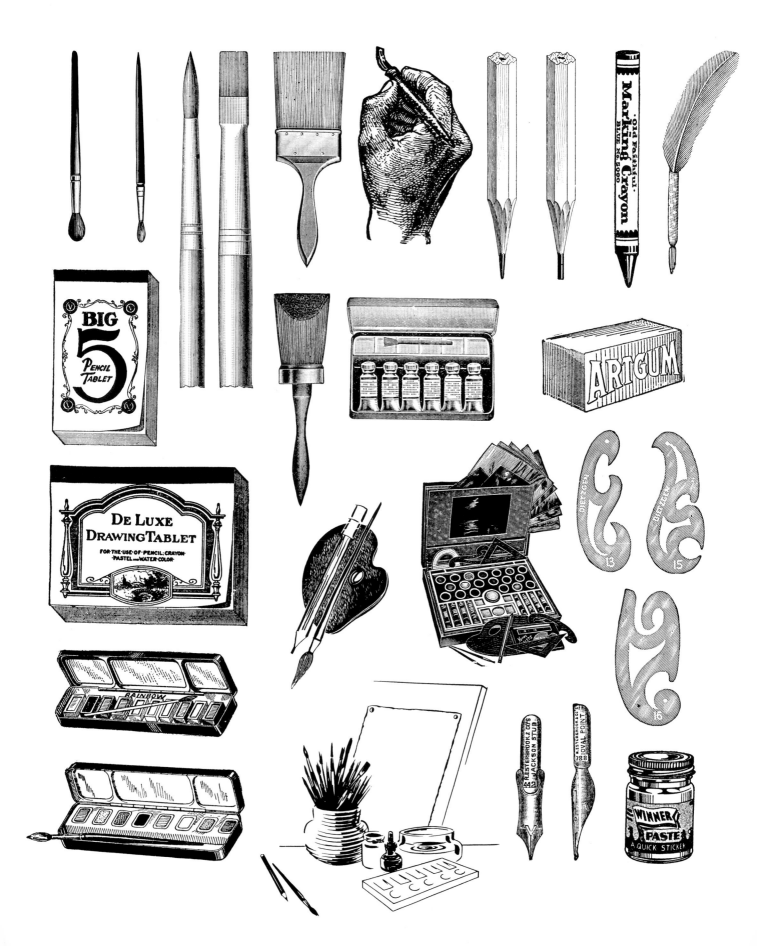

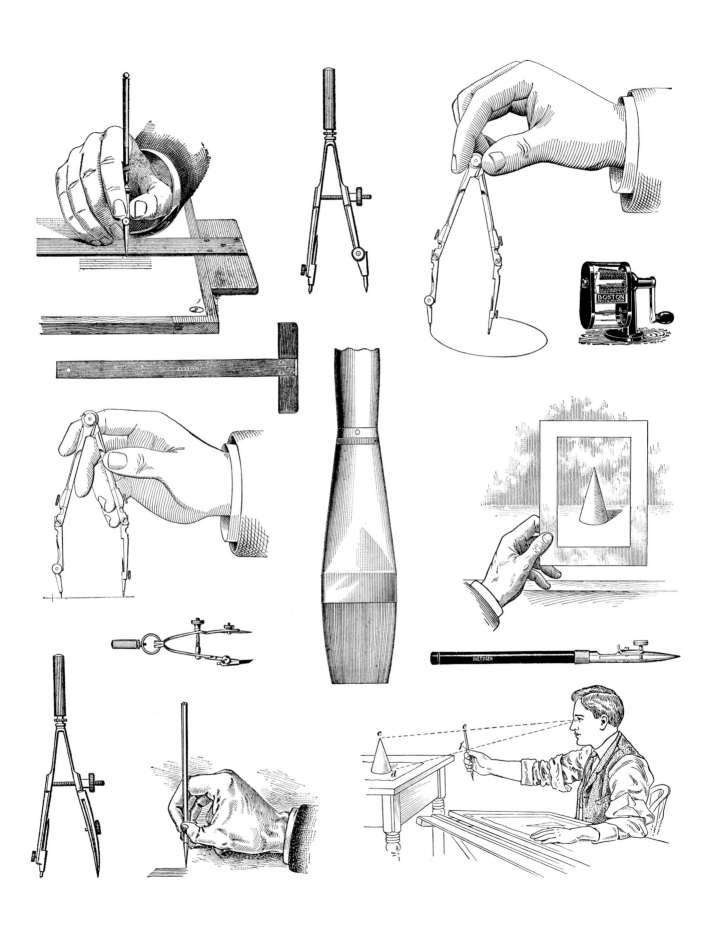

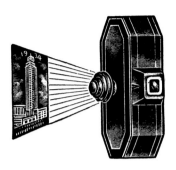

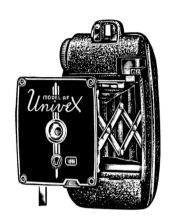

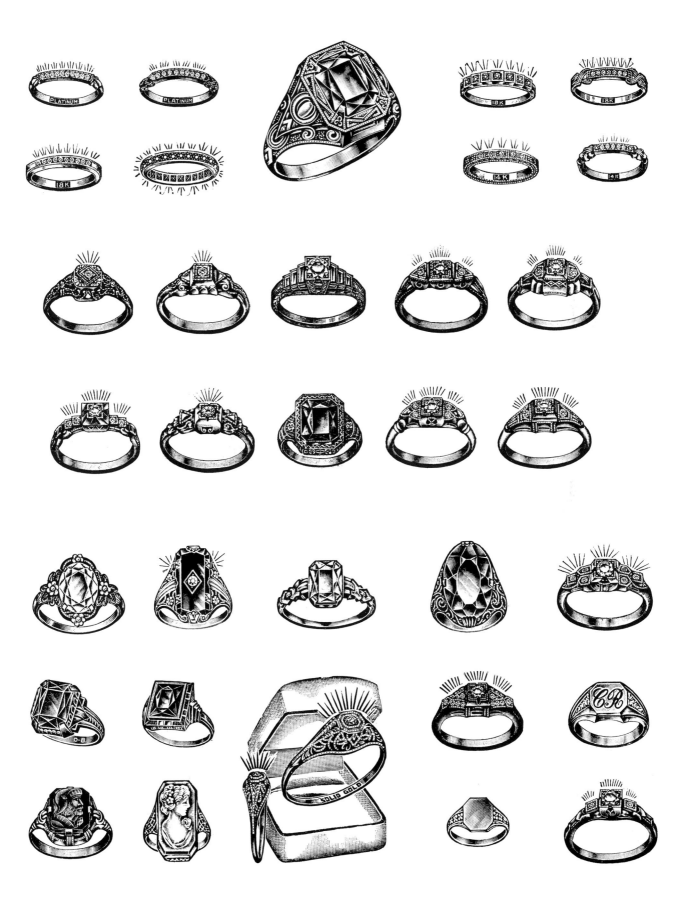

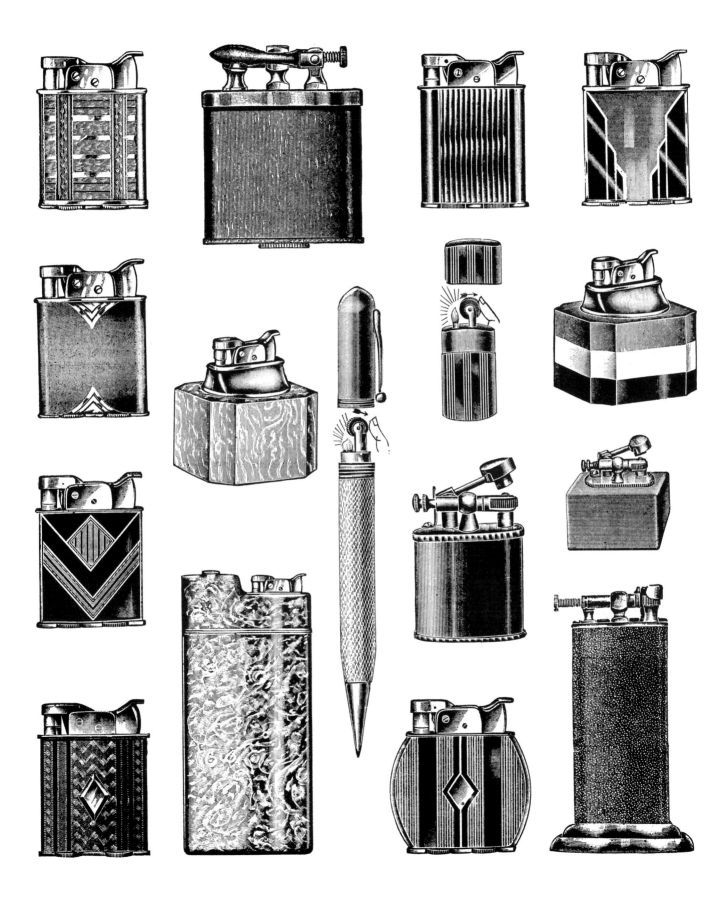

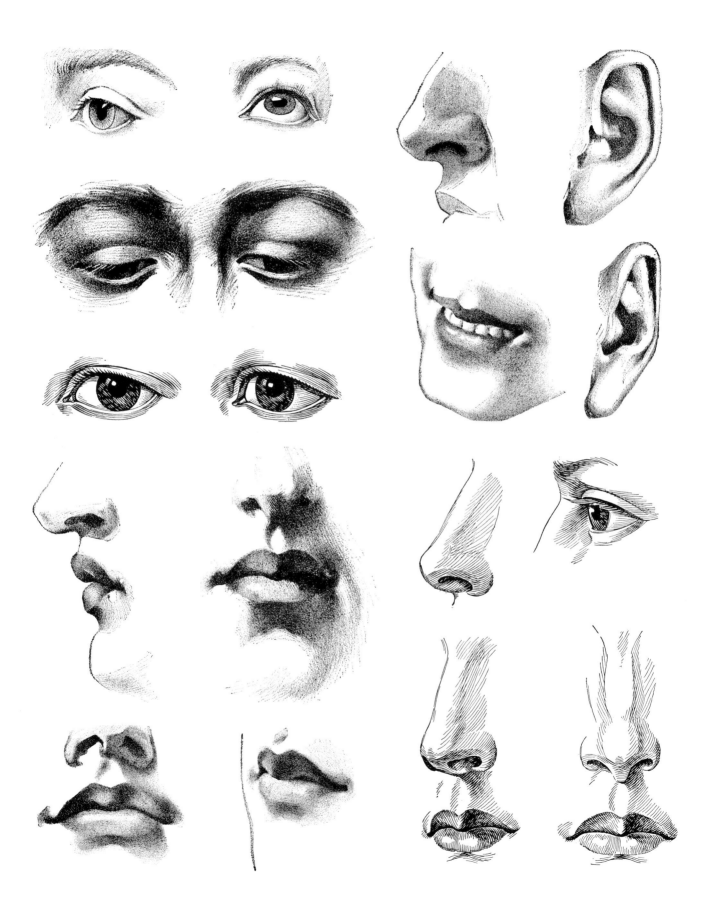

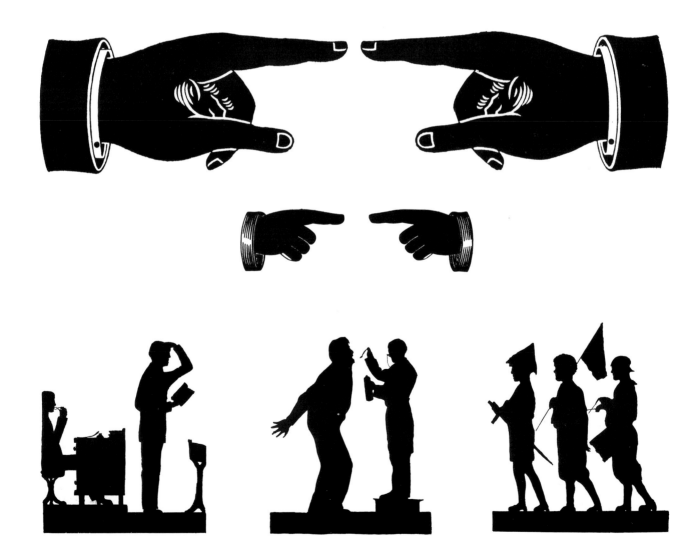

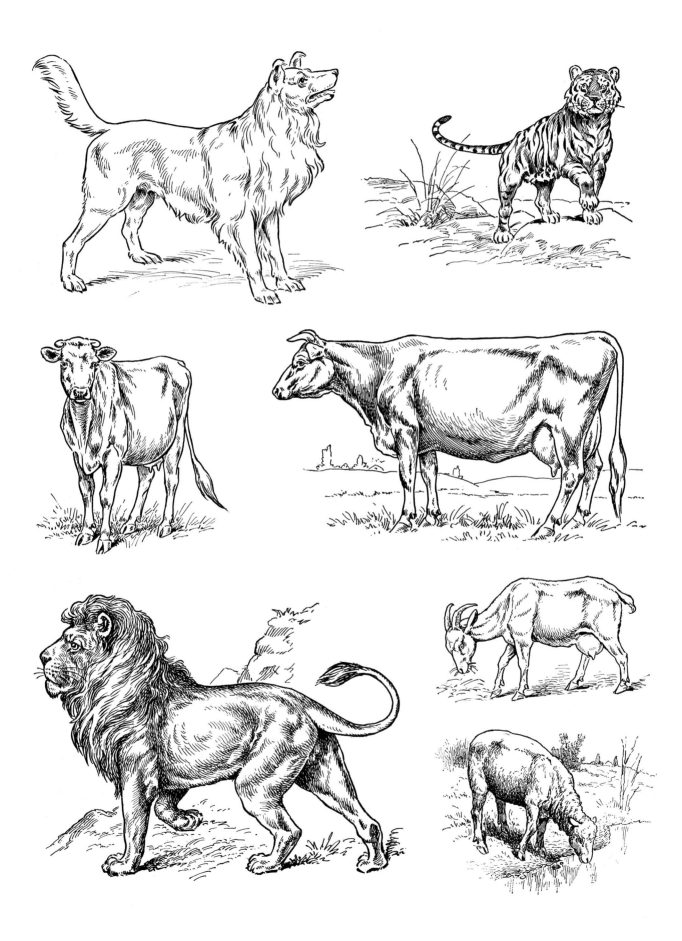

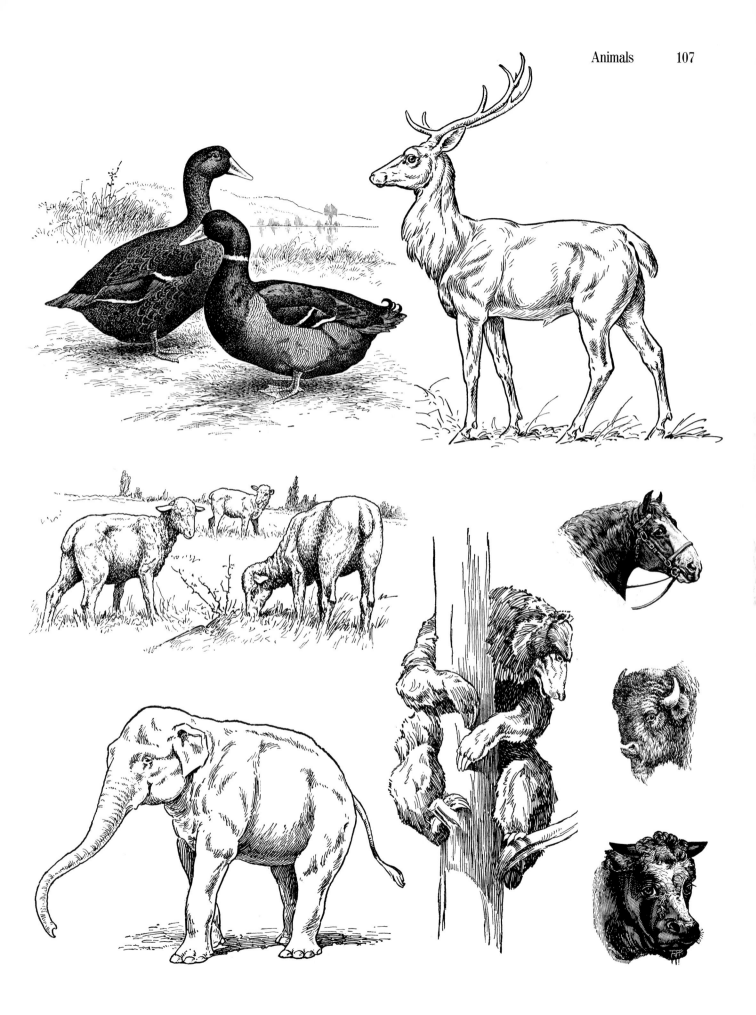

Baby Ruth
Real PEPPERMINT Gum

TURI

JAM

PARCHEESI

FAMOUS CLOWN PUZZLE

LONE STAR RANGER

JUVENILE 268 POLICE

LUCKY PENNY

MATRIMONIAL BOND

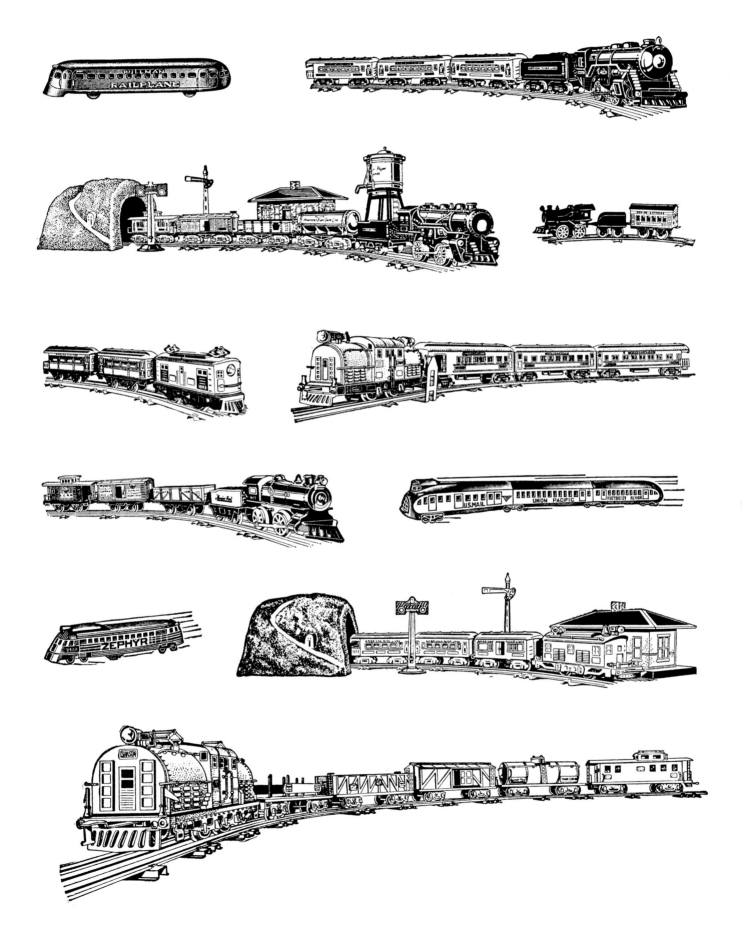

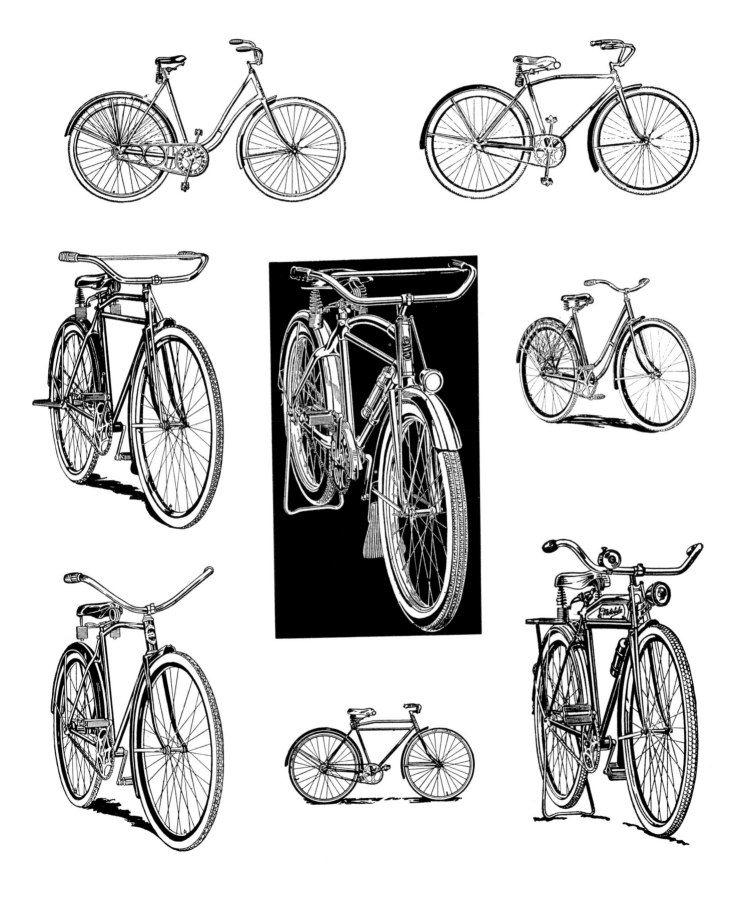

Index